Praise for ROOT

"It is both refreshing and commendable to witness the restoration of these powerful ancestral traditions by the Afro-diaspora. More importantly, McQuillar clarifies the distinction between "Hoodoo," the magio-botanical arts, and Vodoun, the ancestral and deific religion."

—MAMAISSII VIVIAN DANSI HOUNON,
MAMI WATA & ARARA VODOUN PRIESTESS,
PRESIDENT OF MAMI WATA HEALING SOCIETY OF NORTH AMERICA, INC.

"Descendants of African peoples who were brought to the Americas via the slave trade were able to retain their wisdom in places like Cuba and Brazil where the cultural climate allowed them to flourish alongside the dominant Roman Catholic faith. In North America, however, with the possible exception of the New Orleans area, it was thought that the wisdom of the Africans had been eradicated by the less tolerant Protestant mentality of the dominant culture. In her groundbreaking work *Rootwork*, Tayannah Lee McQuillar shows that far from being eradicated, the ancient wisdom of these Africans survives and thrives under the care of Root Doctors, who continue to be an important part of many people's lives. *Rootwork* is a needed book. It presents its subject in an honest, direct, easy-to-understand fashion. Ms. McQuillar successfully reclaims for North American descendants of Africans their rightful place among other similar traditions in the West Indies and Latin America. I thoroughly recommend this book."

—BABA RAUL CANIZARES, AUTHOR, *CUBAN SANTERIA: WALKING WITH THE NIGHT* AND *THE BOOK ON PALO*

"*Rootwork* is a small pocket book jam-packed with loads of information. The basic foundation of rootworking is laid out in an easy-to-understand format. This book will quickly become a guide and reference source for all people who wish to learn this system of folk magick. Hoodoo Doctors and Rootworkers have had great fame in the past in the American South. Here you will learn about divination as it is used by Rootworkers, the history of Rootworking in America, the six common beliefs of Rootworkers, the different types of spirits, and fifty-three spells, all related to traditional Rootworking. Highly recommended and a must-read."

—RAY T. MALBROUGH, AUTHOR OF
CHARMS, SPELLS & FORMULAS AND *THE MAGICAL POWER OF THE SAINTS*

*This book is dedicated to all the Root
Doctors and Spiritualists in the South
who kept the traditions of Africa alive
against all odds. Thank you.*

CONTENTS

CONTENTS

PREFACE

FOR AS LONG as I can remember I have been fascinated with the cultural and spiritual traditions of people around the world. I studied Eastern and Western faiths far and wide, but I was disturbed that I knew little about the folk traditions of African Americans.

For many years I found nothing substantial on Rootwork because it isn't a religion, and when it was mentioned it was simply disregarded as "Negro superstition" and not a serious form of magick (The word *magic* refers to an illusion and indicates charlatanry. *Magick* spelled with a "k" refers to something real that cannot be scientifically proven).

I decided to take a trip to New Orleans, where much of the magio-religious practices of Black America are still intact. I was so excited that when I got back to New York I shared all that I learned with my grandmother. That's when she began telling me stories about an old Rootworker called "Mother."

The woman was called "Mother" as a sign of respect. She was

from South Carolina and had great spiritual powers. My grand-mother would talk for hours about Mother's extraordinary abil-ity to control the outcome of situations. She said that when Mother retired, she could proudly say she never let down a client.

I loved listening to the exciting tales of Mother, but it made me sad that people like her were never given recognition as great shamans. In fact, it is a common belief that African Americans lost most of their magickal ties to Mother Africa through the transatlantic slave holocaust, but nothing can be further from the truth.

Although much of the theology behind the spells has been lost, we've preserved a great deal through a strong oral tradition that continues to this day.

It is for this reason that I want Rootwork and Rootworkers to be put among the ranks of other powerful mystical traditions and given the proper respect they deserve.

Rootwork: Using the Folk Magick of Black America for Love, Money, and Success is my tribute to our almost forgotten wisdom.

Peace and Blessings,
Tayannah Lee McQuillar
New York City, 2002

ACKNOWLEDGMENTS

THANKS TO THE CREATOR for creating the beautiful, bountiful universe in which we live and for allowing me to experience life.

Thanks to my ancestors for without them I would not be here.

Thanks to my family for their boundless love and support.

To my best friend and soul mate, William Sandifer, who for ten years has been my partner on a long and fruitful spiritual journey. Thanks for listening and believing in me.

To my editor, Marcela Landres, for her hard work and for making my dream a reality.

And to all my teachers and friends, a heartfelt thank you.

HOW TO USE THIS BOOK

I HAVE STRUCTURED this book as an accessible guide to African-American folk magick. It is intended for beginners as well as for the advanced practitioner. Don't worry about purchasing every magickal tool or ingredient mentioned in this book right away. You might want to read the sections "Rootwork Basics" and "Elements of Rootwork" prior to using the spells to familiarize yourself with essential principles. The most important thing is to keep an open mind and have fun!

This book is divided into three parts:

Part 1, "**Rootwork Basics**," introduces you to the history and philosophy of Rootwork from its beginnings in Africa to the New World.

Part 2, "**Elements of Rootwork**," is where you'll learn how to use the elements of nature for spells, communicate with ancestors, and create talismans and charms. You'll also learn how to read playing cards to foretell the future.

Part 3, "Understanding Spells for Love, Money, and Success," is where you'll get useful tips on spell casting, as well as the do's and don'ts. You'll also have plenty of sample spells to try to bring love, money, and success into your life.

At the end of the book, you'll find a list of resources to help you learn more, plus a list of magickal suppliers.

ROOTWORK BASICS

WHAT IS ROOTWORK?

ROOTWORK IS A FORM of folk magick that uses the elements of nature to create change in ourselves, others, or our environment. It is an African-American form of shamanism that makes use of herbs, stones, rocks, and other organic material to heal the body or the mind, or to solve a problem. Like all other forms of shamanism, Rootworkers believe that we can use the unseen forces of nature to manipulate the tangible world.

Rootwork is also known as "Hoodoo" in the southern part of the United States. The word *Hoodoo* is probably derived from the word *juju*, an African word meaning "magic," or from *Voodoo*, a corrupted version of the Fon word *Vodun*, meaning "spirit" or "god." But unlike Vodun, Lukumi, Candomble, Shango, Batque, etc., Rootwork is not a religion. It has no pantheon or priesthood. It refers only to a set of healing and spell practices, and the practitioner can be whatever religion they wish. The theology behind the spells has been lost, thus there are no formal initiations to become a Rootworker. However, a good practitioner is traditionally referred to as Doctor, Mother, Uncle, or Aunt out of respect for their vast problem-solving knowledge.

Prior to the great migration of blacks to urban cities, these shamans were equally feared and respected, and usually lived away from the "regular folks" and made a profitable business off people who would sneak to see them under the cloak of darkness for help in resolving their issues. Most people lived by the saying "You want salvation, go to church. You want something done, go to the Rootworker."

Rootwork also served a practical purpose in the black community. Many Africans had experience working with herbs in their homeland and transmitted their botanical knowledge to their children. This information was passed on orally and was used to cure the sick and ailing. The most common afflictions Rootworkers treated were smallpox and digestive disorders, by boiling down the roots of certain herbs like the spikenard (hyptis suaveolens) or the sensitive plant (mimosa pudica) and making a tonic for their clients to drink.

All blacks in the South had to know basic healing techniques because traditional health care was too expensive for slaves to afford. In fact, many whites couldn't afford a traditional doctor either, and would often turn to their slaves' botanical knowledge for cures.

NATIVE AMERICANS AND ROOTWORK

African slaves would often seek refuge among Native Americans because they had a similar worldview and they were willing to teach them how to survive in the New World. Although Africans were knowledgeable about African plants and their uses, they had no idea what to do with the herbs found in this strange land. Native Americans taught them the properties of local herbs and roots. The depiction of Native American chiefs and warriors on the packages of many "luck drawing" floor washes are testimony to the impact Native Americans had on rootwork.

These floor washes are simply a combination of water mixed with different perfumes and contain no herbs or roots at all. Most people don't read the ingredients in these products but just assume their effectiveness because of the clever packaging. Certainly if there is an image of a Native American on it, the product must be "magical," right? When, in fact, it's about as magical as Mop-n-Glow.

ROOTWORK TODAY

When African Americans migrated north, many left Rootwork behind. They were seeking better opportunities and a more sophisticated way of living, and Rootwork was considered "backward" or "country" and was frowned upon. This theme was dealt with in Julie Dash's cinematic masterpiece, *Daughters of the Dust.*

As standard medical care became more available, fewer people had need for the Rootworkers. But many still consulted them to perform divination or spell work.

Today, because of miseducation and the media's negative portrayal of any spiritual system based in Africa, most people avoid Rootwork. Everything that is African is feared, ignored, and rejected because of a deep and painful history of erasure of Africa as a major contributor to world culture. Even with the vast knowledge accumulated in the last century, when most people think of African spirituality and its practices in the New World, the mind usually conjures up images of spooky witchdoctors, bloody cannibalistic rituals, and evil curses. The media still transmits this propaganda through cartoons and movies, especially in the horror genre such as *The Serpent and the Rainbow, Child's Play, Voodoo Dawn,* and *Tales from the Crypt* to name a few.

A case in point is Webster's dictionary definition of *Hoodoo:*

Hoodoo: 1. voodoo 2. bad luck 3. A person or thing that brings bad luck.

Inaccuracies such as this pervade our culture, resulting not only in a negative psychological effect on African Americans and others in the Diaspora, but also in preventing others from understanding the true nature of these practices. This book is an attempt to correct these inaccuracies by placing Rootwork in its proper historical, cultural, and spiritual context.

HISTORY OF ROOTWORK

ROOTWORK HAS ITS ORIGINS with the descendants of slaves transported from Africa during the transatlantic slave holocaust. Millions of Africans were transported to the sugar and cotton plantations in North America, South America, and the Caribbean to provide free labor for wealthy European planters. A conservative estimate is that a half million captives were exported to the United States over a course of two hundred years, primarily from the West Coast of the African continent.

Despite the cruel, oppressive nature of slavery and the pressures to assimilate, African traditions survived. Many scholars have argued that they didn't in North America, due to the particularly brutal nature of slavery in the United States, which was much harsher than in South America or the Caribbean.

In South America and on the islands, slaves were allowed to congregate, which made it much easier for them to maintain their religious practices. Many of them could mask their ancient gods behind a barrage of saints. Africans would correlate certain characteristics of Catholic saints to the deities they worshipped at home. For example, in Cuba, Saint Barbara with the red robe, crown, and brandished sword became a perfect mask for the Yoruba god of war, Shango. Thus, if slave owners saw an altar to Saint Barbara, they would not become suspicious and Africans could continue to worship their gods without the fear of being penalized. In addition, the climate was warmer, making it easier to escape to the hills and mountains to practice their traditions.

In the United States, slaves were not allowed to hold meetings of any kind other than to attend church. Their masters were Protestant, which made it difficult to disguise their deities. In Protestantism there weren't any saints to hide behind or even a goddess-figure to emulate in the form of Mary. This was particularly devastating to the survival of African spirituality in America since Africans have always held the feminine aspect of God in high esteem. This is how the African religions were lost in the United States. The exception is Louisiana, which had a strong Catholic base left behind by French colonists, thus making it easier for blacks to hide their African loa (gods) from the Vodun (Voodoo) tradition behind the saints. However, it wasn't so easy for African Americans to forget the vast magickal and herbal knowledge they had. Thus, Rootwork was born.

ROOTWORK AND POPULAR CULTURE

In the beginning of the twentieth century, Rootwork was a main topic of many rhythm and blues songs. At the time, blues music was only intended for a black audience, and was known as race music. It wasn't until the 1940s, when whites began to listen to it and white musicians began to play it, that the term was changed to the more friendly rhythm and blues. Because most whites weren't listening, the musicians of the time felt comfortable singing about whatever they wanted. This tradition continued until the late seventies (an example is Muddy Waters' hit "I Got My Mojo Workin'") but didn't survive the integration of music in the melting pot of the eighties. Performers such as Bessie Smith, Lightnin' Hopkins, Ida Cox, Robert Johnson, Muddy Waters, Charley Patton, Big Joe Williams, and Screamin' Jay Hawkins sang about mojos, hot foot powder, curses, and famous Rootworkers they knew such as Aunt Caroline Dye and the Seven Sisters of New Orleans.

As art is the biggest testimony to the culture of all people, Rootwork was and is a rich part of our heritage that is now looked down upon or forgotten.

ROOTWORK IN THE TWENTY-FIRST CENTURY

Because of the lack of familiarity that many African Americas have with their African heritage and the increasing emphasis on merging into a single "world culture," it is now difficult for them and other ethnic groups to maintain their identity. The solution is to re-educate ourselves and our children so we will not have to look outside of ourselves for cultures to identify with.

WHY DO ROOTWORK?

1. To honor the ancient wisdom of our ancestors. It is our cultural heritage and a cherished link to our past.

2. As a means to get back to loving the Earth and respecting nature, so that we will stop killing the environment, her creatures, and ourselves.

3. For self-empowerment and spiritual growth.

4. To reconnect with who and what we are and get our families back together.

5. Because it's beautiful.

HOW DOES IT WORK?

NO FORM OF MAGICK is based on logic—if it was, then it would cease to be magick. There is no explanation for why spells work, but they do. All that is needed to work successfully with spells is patience, confidence, and faith. It is a completely illogical process that must be allowed simply to be. As soon as you try to analyze it, its power is lost. It is natural to wonder why things happen, but God has made it so no matter how many answers we find to a question there will be more in its place, thus maintaining the mystery of the universe. For example, we know that water is composed of two elements of hydrogen and one element of oxygen, yet despite this knowledge scientists can't "create" water.

Believe in the mysteries of the universe and know you are part of the same strength, magnificence, and beauty that makes a flower bloom, a volcano erupt, and the sun rise. Our ancestors knew and understood this. Let's explore their beliefs.

◯◯SIX COMMON BELIEFS OF ROOTWORKERS

1. There Is One God

Most Rootworkers believe in one God that we must ultimately answer to for all of our actions. However, it is believed that underneath that supreme God exists many supernatural forces such as angels, ancestors, etc. that can be conjured to intercede on the behalf of humans. Traditionally, most Rootworkers were Christians, but it is important to note that Rootwork in no way conflicted with the beliefs of the church in the minds of the people. It merely supplemented the religious beliefs to which they adhered. It was believed by Africans that if two things are good, you shouldn't have to choose which is better.

2. The Earth Is Sacred

To Rootworkers the Earth is a living, breathing entity and is sacred. It is from the Earth that we get all of our materials to perform our works, and it is our home. It is of great importance to the Rootworker to honor the Earth by leaving offerings periodically out of respect for the forces of nature. That is why they don't take dirt, rocks, or shells without leaving something first. This practice has been misunderstood by many as a primitive act when in fact it symbolizes humility and appreciation for forces beyond our comprehension.

3. Physical Death Is Not Final

The Rootworker acknowledges that physical death is not final and that the soul of a person is eternal and therefore can be communicated with. It is believed that the spirits of the dead have the extraordinary power to impart wisdom on the living because they have passed on to a spiritual plane where the past, present, and the future are one.

4. The Future Can Be Foretold

Rootworkers rely heavily on divination to foretell the futures of their clients. Playing cards, bones, shells, dream interpretation, and especially the ability to recognize omens in nature were highly prized skills. The practice of reading omens in nature was lost in the 1930s during the great migration of African Americans from the rural South to the more urban North. The spiritual or psychic reading remains one of the most popular forms of divination. This usually involves the use of a candle and a glass of water to "read" the client.

5. The Right to Self-Defense and Retaliation

Rootworkers believe they have a right to defend themselves and/or retaliate against their enemies and generally don't adhere to the traditional notion of Karma. However, they do believe that the punishment must fit the crime, and anything else beyond that is subject to negative repercussions.

6. Honesty and Confidentiality

It was and is one of the greatest crimes for a Rootworker to cheat a client for personal gain. The Rootworker's ability is viewed as a great gift—one has been "called" to be of aid to others just as a priest or nun is called to join the Catholic Church. Cheating a client is seen no differently from a medical doctor who purposely misleads a patient, and is believed to be just as dangerous. Rootworkers who did this were referred to as "Black Gypsies" and were rare. An honest Rootworker would tell the client if they could not perform a work for them, no matter what the client offered. It is also of equal importance that Rootworkers keep all client information extremely confidential, as sharing personal information with others is unacceptable.

ELEMENTS OF ROOTWORK II

ELEMENTS OF ROOTWORK

ALTHOUGH ROOTWORK HAS NO religious structure, it still functions as a very powerful magickal system with rules and taboos that are strictly observed. The elements of Rootwork are primarily focused on the understanding and mastery of using natural and supernatural forces to solve everyday problems such as financial or relationship trouble. The emphasis of this system is on self-empowerment and warding off negative energy through the use of charms, talismans, cleansing baths, and ritual work.

ELEMENTAL MAGICK

Air, earth, fire, and water. These are the four elements from which everything on this planet is composed. In Rootwork, it is important to learn how to use, or "work," these forces for maximum results in magickal endeavors. Since they are the very foundation of the concrete world, it is important to understand the principles they represent.

The concept of elemental magick is as old as humanity itself. Prehistoric man used to literally worship the world around him, in awe of its mysteries. A Rootworker must have this essential love and respect for nature in order to perfect their craft. This may be difficult if you live in an artificial world full of manicured lawns, skyscrapers, and cement pavements, but it can be done. In the following pages I will discuss the four elements and how they relate to Rootwork.

AIR

Incense is used in Rootwork to represent the air element. It is believed that incense is pleasing to spirits and carries wishes to heaven. Incense is most often used to purify, set a mood, or produce a particular vibration in a given space. It has been used since ancient times for these purposes and it still is widely used as an essential component of the religious services of many Eastern and Western traditions. Here is a list of traditional incenses and their uses in Rootwork.

INCENSE	PURPOSE
Anise	Psychic awareness Increase occult power
Bayberry	Draws money Prosperity
Camphor	Eliminates evil spirits Brain stimulant Purification
Cinnamon	Sexuality/sensuality Harmony Love
Eucalyptus	Courage Increase sexual desire Protection
Frankincense	Purification Spirit Communication
Jasmine	Strengthens intuition Intensifies dreams Promotes sensitivity

Mint	Clarity Openness Cleansing
Myrrh	Stability Focus Provokes deep thought
Rose	Joy Love Peace
Sage	Meditation Purification

EARTH

The Earth is a living, breathing entity and like any other living thing, it absorbs and gives off energy. This is the fundamental reason why Rootworkers collect earth from various locations. It is believed that using certain kinds of earth "grounds" a spell. I must remind you that if you take a handful of earth, you should leave an offering out of respect. Notice that I didn't use the term "dirt," as it has a negative connotation. Many people in African-based traditions use earth from certain places as an enhancer. The most common use of earth is in a mojo bag. The earth is placed in a small bag with other ingredients and the bag is worn against the skin.

LOCATION OF EARTH	PURPOSE
Bank	For money and success, use the earth surrounding a bank. If possible, go to a popular bank and collect it.
Cemetery	To stimulate psychic ability or to strengthen communication with the dead.
Church	For spiritual protection and to ward against evil spirits.
Courthouse	For success in legal matters.
Garden	For love spells, use earth from a beautiful garden.
Hospital	To cure the sick or ailing.
Jail	To keep the police away, when someone is having trouble with the law.
Marketplace	For money and employment spells, use earth surrounding a busy marketplace.
Mountain	To increase psychic abilities and clarity. If possible, use the earth from the top of a high mountain.
Police station	For protection from enemies. *Do not* use if you are involved in any illegal activity.

FIRE

Candles are used in Rootwork, as in other magickal systems, to represent the fire element. Candles give power to our desires and intentions by concentrating our energies while it is lit as well as afterward. We can still feel the effects of heat long after its source has been extinguished, and so it is with magick. All things supernatural follow the same laws found in nature.

CANDLE COLORS AND MEANINGS

COLOR	PURPOSE
Black	Absorb negativity Increase occult power Cause a hex Promote change
Blue	Healing Insight Improves psychic ability
Brown	Stability Money Focus
Gold	Prosperity Fame

Green	Money
	Abundance
	Growth
Gray	Promotes balance
	Eases the pain of grief
Orange	Clarity
	Energy
Pink	Attraction
	Healing
	Joy
Purple	Spirituality
	Humility
Red	Desire
	Strength
	Power
Silver	Awakens intuition
	Improves psychic ability
	Eases stress
White	All-purpose
	Lit in honor of the dead
	Peace
Yellow	Creativity
	Optimism
	Renewal

How to Interpret Candle Phenomena

Candle phenomena refers to how the candle's flame behaves after it has been lit. It is believed that a candle communicates via its flame.

PHENOMENON	MEANING
Repeatedly goes out	A sign. Try again after twenty-four hours. If it happens again, throw the candle away and do not try to perform the spell. It isn't the right time.
Low flame	The candle may be trying to give forth the energy to achieve your objective but is "weighed down" psychically. Say a prayer to reinforce your purpose and the flame may grow. A low flame can also be a very positive sign; a calm before the storm of sorts. Monitor its growth and see what happens.
Flickering	A very good sign. All of the energy you have put into your prayer or spell has been absorbed and is going to work.
Crackling noises/Sparks	This is an excellent sign. Guaranteed success.
Double/Multiple flames	Sometimes when burning a seven-day candle, the wick will fold over and develop into two or even three separate flames. This is a very auspicious sign because it is believed a spiritual guide is aiding you with a spell. Try not to put out a candle that does this.
Glass breaks	If you are burning a seven-day candle and the glass breaks, throw it out immediately. It means that whatever has been preventing you from getting what you want has been removed.

Reading Candle Wax

This technique applies to plain candles, not seven-day candles that are contained in glass. Reading candle wax is a form of divination used to foretell the success or failure of, or to receive a message about your spell. For example, if the wax forms an image of what looks like a snake and you fear snakes, you should take note and think about how it relates to your spell. Remember, nothing you see is bad. What you see is simply a message that your unconscious mind is trying to send *you*. Another person might see the same image and interpret it in a different way, or they might even see a completely different image. Their interpretation is irrelevant, because the candle is intended to be interpreted by you and you alone. For instance, if you see a snake after doing a spell for employment, it may mean you need to use cunning methods to get the job you want. Write down how you feel about a particular object or image to gather meanings. If you can't think of anything, refer to a dream dictionary for help.

Here are ten of the most common wax images and what they mean.

1. Angels.

You must turn to a spiritual guide for help with your situation. This can also be a reminder for you from neglected guides to get your attention.

2. Cup.

You will be receiving an answer soon regarding your spell. You will most likely know when this answer appears, and you should follow it even if it's something you don't want to do.

3. Face.

An ancestor is attempting to help you with your spell.

4. Flower.

Your spell will come to fruition. It may also mean that you will not want whatever you have asked for in the long run.

5. Hand.

You may need to seek assistance from someone more experienced. You might not be spiritually strong enough to do the spell you attempted.

6. Bird.

Usually a sure sign of success.

7. Musical Instrument.

Usually a sign that you've overdone a spell.

8. Heart.

If you see a heart after doing a love spell it means the spell will be successful. For other spells it may mean that you didn't think things through before you acted.

9. Animal.

It is common to see animals in wax. The meaning depends on the type of animal and the type of spell. For example, you might see an eagle and interpret that to indicate success in business.

10. Tree.

Usually guarantees success, though patience may be required before what you are seeking becomes manifest.

WATER

Water is a very powerful element because it is receptive. It is the ultimate retainer of energy and is often used to cleanse a person or space, or to consecrate an object. To attain the various types of waters requires patience and preparation.

WATER	PURPOSE
War water	For revenge or to place a hex. War water is prepared by taking two cups of water from a heavy thunderstorm and filling a 32 oz. jar or a bottle until it's half full. Add nine rusty nails, brimstone (sulphur), and a little of your urine. Store the container in a cool, dry place until ready for use. It is commonly thrown on the front door of the intended victim.
Peace water	To bring peace and positive spiritual vibrations into the home. Usually made by mixing half a cup of Florida Water perfume, three cups of holy water, eight fresh or dried basil leaves, and three crushed eggshells. It is commonly used as a floor wash. Add twice the ingredients for a larger room.
Ocean	Bathe in the water of the ocean for peace of mind. Add a little to your regular bathwater every night if you're trying to conceive. Dab a little on the center of your forehead (third eye) in a clockwise, circular motion before divination to increase psychic abilities. The third eye is an energy center or chakra associated with spiritual awakening.
River	Consecrate sacred objects for added blessings. Mix it with cinnamon and mop the floors with it for money and luck.

First spring rain	Sprinkle around the house for joy the whole year round. Wash your face and hair with it to remain youthful. Rub on your stomach for fertility and healing. Wash mojo bags with it for luck. Many people who use this spell place a glass bowl out on the windowsill on March 21st (Spring equinox) until the first spring rain.
Full moon water	Prepare moon water by leaving a glass bowl of tap or spring water out in the full moonlight overnight. Rub on the back of your neck and forehead every nine days to increase psychic ability. Wash your hair with it to stimulate growth. Bathe in it for fertility. Keep a glass of it by your bed for clearer dreams.
Holy water	Use to consecrate sacred objects. Sprinkle around the home to dispense negativity. Clean your eyes with it for clarity.
Storm water	Place a bowl of plain tap or spring water out on the windowsill and wait until the next storm. Sprinkle on a luck mojo bag to enhance its potential. Sprinkle around the home for desired change. *Do not* handle if you're sick. Sweeten the water with a pinch of brown sugar for a money mojo bag.

TALISMANS AND CHARMS

ROOTWORK MAKES USE of a wide range of talismans and charms to attract good luck or protect the person for whom they are made. They are usually prepared with fresh or dried herbs and roots, depending on the client's objective. Once the charm has been consecrated using one of the waters or incense described previously, it is advised that no one else handle it except the person it was intended for. Here is a list of the most common ingredients used in Rootwork talismans:

Angelica root:
Protection and to remove a hex (uncrossing).

Badger tooth:
Carried for good luck.

Black cat bone:
Increase psychic development or to create a jinx.

Black-eyed peas:
Good luck. Place three in a mojo bag with one of each silver coin.

Buckeye nut:
Attract money.

Chicken nail:
The nail off the foot of a chicken is considered good luck when it's placed in a mojo bag for money.

Coffin nails:
Nails from a coffin are used to jinx or cause trouble.

Corn kernels:
Probably Native American influence. Used in money spells.

Currency:
Attracts more money when included in a mojo bag with magnetic sand and a tonka bean.

Devil's Shoestring (viburnum alnifolium):
Also called cramp bark. This is an herb in the honeysuckle family. The root of this plant looks like shoelaces, thus its strange name. Good luck for gamblers, protection, or to find a job.

Dragon's Blood Ink:

Enhances any spell that must be written on paper.

Dried bat:

Increase psychic development, jinx, or protection.

Feathers:

Enhancer of any spell, depending on the bird it is taken from.

- Buzzard for jinx
- Crane for health
- Crow for psychic ability
- Dove for peace

Five Finger Grass (potentilla canadensis):

Also called cinquefoil. The root of this herb resembles a human hand, thus earning its name. Used for gambling and protection.

Four leaf clover:

Carried for good luck.

Gator foot:

Good luck for gamblers or protection. Usually worn on a key chain.

Gator head:

Protection. Usually hung in the home by the front door. Common in Louisiana.

Goofer dust (same as graveyard dust):

Used to cause harm, trouble, or to kill an enemy. From the Kikongo word *Kufwa* which means "to die."

Gunpowder:

A common ingredient in hexes. Can cause extremely bad luck when mixed with goofer dust. For good it can be used as an enhancer to luck spells.

Horseshoe:

Good luck.

Hot foot powder (an equal mixture of red pepper, black pepper, sulphur, and salt):

Sprinkled around a person's doorstep to make an enemy move away. Today it is used by Rootworkers in the workplace and sprinkled in front of the client's office or around their desk.

High John the Conqueror root:

Love, strength, and money. Usually carried in the pocket or purse.

Lodestone:

Attract whatever you want.

Magnetic sand (ground iron filings):

Attract whatever you want. Usually prepared with Buckeye nut or lodestone and placed in a mojo bag.

Rabbit's foot:

Good luck.

Rue (ruta graveolens):

Leaves from this plant protect a person from the evil eye when placed in a mojo bag.

Snakeskin:

Increase psychic development, jinx, or protection.

Stones:

Rocks and stones are believed to carry the spirit of the Earth and are used to "ground" a spell.

Tonka bean (dipteryx odorata):

This aromatic bean is in the vanilla family and is said to attract good luck and money. Throw in running water after making a wish.

Wishbone:

Good luck.

MOJO BAGS

A mojo bag is a tiny bag made of flannel, silk, or leather that includes herbs, stones, and other ingredients combined to achieve an objective. It is the most popular talisman in Rootwork and is also called a gris-gris, wanga, conjure, or trick bag. The word *mojo* is probably a corrupted version of the Yoruba/West African word *mojuba*, which means "giving praise." They are usually worn against the skin or carried in a pocket or purse and should always remain hidden. It is believed that if someone else touches your mojo it will lose its potency, so keep it safely out of sight.

Some mojo bags come already prepared in occult shops or botanicas (shops that specialize in tools for practitioners of African traditional religions), but it is recommended that you personalize it with your own hair or fingernail clippings. You may also write a wish or prayer on a piece of brown paper bag and place it inside the mojo. The prayer should be written in pencil to ground it with the power of lead. After the mojo is prepared, it should be consecrated with incense, cigar, or candle smoke by "baptizing" it in fumes, or anointed with a magical oil (rose for love, gardenia protection, etc.), rum, or holy water. If you plan to concoct your own bag, remember to put an odd number of ingredients into it, never even. An even number of ingredients is considered bad luck in a gris-gris, unless it is to be used to hex someone. Mojo bags should be red for passion, green or gold for money or luck, pink for love, or purple for psychic ability.

OTHER TALISMANS

Nation sack:

Same as a mojo bag but it is only prepared by women for women. Usually used to keep a mate faithful or to attract a lover. It is believed that if a man touches it the power of the sack is destroyed.

Seals:

Rootworkers began using seals in the middle of the twentieth century as a direct influence from the Jewish magickal system of Kabbala. The seals depict an elaborate design that represent the planets, elements, saints, angels, and demons. They are similar in appearance to the Veves (mandalas) used in Haitian Vodou to call the spirits, which are drawn on the ground in cornmeal. Seals can be found in *The Sixth and Seventh Book of Moses* by the Egyptian Publishing Co. (Kessinger Publishing Co.) and either traced onto parchment or cut right out. They are carried in a wallet or placed in a mojo bag that fits the objective.

Crystals/ Gemstones:

Traditionally, Rootworkers couldn't afford crystals and gemstones but they did believe in their power. Now that they are more affordable, modern Rootworkers now study the mystical powers of minerals and use them in a wide range of spell craft. All crystals and gemstones should be cleaned by running them under cold water, then leaving them in the moon or sunlight or in a bowl of sea salt and water overnight.

Invocations:

Spoken charms or invocations are almost never used in Rootwork because it has no liturgy of its own. Chants, songs, etc. are common in Wicca and other forms of shamanism, but Rootworkers never had the opportunity because they worked alone in secret most of the time. Rootworkers also believe that objects in nature are inherently powerful and do not need to be "energized" through song and prayer. The most that was said was the Lord's Prayer, or in New Orleans the Hail Mary because the city was predominantly Catholic.

INGREDIENTS USED FROM THE HUMAN BODY

It is common for Rootworkers to use secretions, skin, or hair for spells. They believe they carry a person's essence and would make a spell work stronger. Modern science has confirmed this with the discovery of DNA. Ingredients from the body are most commonly used to dominate or keep a mate faithful as a form of pheremone magick to mark your territory.

Feces:

Mostly used for hexes. Place the photograph or name of your

victim in a jar with a lid and put your feces in it. Seal it tightly and bury it in their yard or a cemetery.

Hair:

A small amount of someone's hair can be used as a jinx. There are many hexes associated with hair but the most common method was to steal a person's hair from a comb or brush, spit on it, and throw it in a bird's nest. It is said that this will eventually drive a person crazy. Another domination spell is to sprinkle your pubic hair occasionally into your lover's food to keep them faithful.

Menstrual Blood:

Women have the most occult power during their period. Blood is considered "hot," so a female Rootworker will only prepare "hot" spells or gris-gris when menstruating for maximum effect. "Hot" spells deal with love, revenge, attraction, or sex magick. Many women put a little menstrual blood in their mate's coffee or tea to entice them, or in their food to keep them faithful. This is also very common in Strega, the Italian system of magick. In Sicily, men avoid eating spaghetti or any saucy foods prepared by unmarried women for fear of being "worked." Menstrual blood can also be used to attract a new lover by placing a drop of it in your favorite perfume.

Nails:

Clipped finger or toenails are used in mojo bags or dolls to personalize them.

Saliva:

Spit can be used to hex or bless depending on what was said right before. I've seen many Haitians use this method of spitting right after cussing somebody out as they walked past. It is said that the person will have bad luck for up to three days after.

Semen:

Men can use their seed to keep a woman faithful by putting it in their food. Another method is to wipe it over the threshold of the door. If she cheats, he will find out quickly. Women can keep a man faithful by stealing a used condom after sex, tying it up, and placing it in a bottle under the bed where he won't see it. He won't be able to look at another woman without thinking of her. Semen mixed with goofer dust will cause a man to go impotent if he tries to have sex with someone else.

Skin:

Scraping the bottom of the foot after a good soak will produce dead skin cells. This is used to dominate or jinx somebody by baking it into their food. Most people use this to gain a promotion at work or to make themselves popular.

Urine:

The most common use for urine is to sprinkle it lightly on a magickal object to personalize it or to break a hex. It is very common for women to wash their doorsteps with their urine to protect themselves from enemies.

LAYING DOWN TRICKS

There are several ways to conceal or dispose of magickal objects, depending on the purpose of the work. In Rootwork this is referred to as "laying down a trick." Materials should always be handled as quickly and discreetly as possible.

Building structure:

Many Rootworkers would lay a trick in a construction site so that it would last forever or at least for as long as the building being constructed stands. To attract money, lay a trick at a bank construction site; to keep the law at bay lay it at a courthouse; for protection lay it at a church.

Crossroads:

Dropping coins or a wanga in the middle of a crossroad is considered extremely lucky as it disperses in all directions. It is also a good place to dispose of a bad luck trick by letting cars run over it, and this causes no harm to the innocent.

Fire:

Burning a jinx in a fire and scattering the ashes around a tree is a quick way to destroy it. Burning a prayer or wish and burying the ashes near home is also common. The same can be done for bad wishes scattered around the doorstep of an enemy.

Graveyard:

Used to "bury" enemies or ritual objects used to cause trouble or harm to another.

Home or yard:

Burial of a trick in the earth allows it to keep working and grounds it. Many people used to bury good luck mojos in their backyard or underneath the front steps or under a plank on their porch. The area around a home or yard could also be used to hex an enemy by waiting till they weren't home and burying a bad luck trick in their yard. If someone had lots of bad luck they would have their dog sniff out the trick and immediately pee on it to destroy it. Women would bury the dirty underwear of their mate to keep them faithful. Mojos are also kept under carpets or rugs in the corners of modern homes.

Powders in food or drink:

Usually magickal powders are used to keep a mate faithful or in other domination spells.

Running water:

It is believed that benevolent spirits reside near streams, lakes, etc., and the water is used to cleanse a trick of any negative energy it might have picked up if it accidently is touched. Throwing a mojo filled with hot foot powder in the opposite direction of your enemy would certainly cause them to move away quickly.

Clothing:

Mojo bags are often sewn into the clothes of the owner so they can be always worn against the skin. Mojos are also sewn into pillowcases, mattresses, and the drape of curtains.

Toilet:

To cleanse yourself spiritually it is common to pass a whole white egg all over your body and aura, break it in the toilet, and flush it. This was done by couples to break any psychic ties to any previous sexual partners. It is also common to defecate into the toilet, write your enemy's name down, and flush it together with their hair as a hex.

Tree:

It is believed that trees and plants in general absorb negative energy, so negative tricks and old mojos are buried at the base of trees to be neutralized. It is common now for Rootworkers to ritually prepare a desk plant by dabbing the leaves lightly with magickal oils or powders for protection or good

TAYANNAH LEE MCQUILLAR

luck. Hexing is also done by giving your enemy a jinxed plant as a gift. This is usually accomplished by sprinkling war water on the leaves or placing a little hot foot powder in the soil. Another old practice is sticking bottles on thin branches of trees after making wishes. It is believed that you will get what you desire. The bottles are also a protection talisman with origins in the African Congo.

SYMBOLS

In case a person is not willing or able to consult a Rootworker, or if the work is against another person, it is possible to use a symbol of the absent party. Photographs and personal objects of the person are often used. Even today, in many parts of Africa and other parts of the world where folk beliefs remain strong, many people will not allow strangers to take their picture for fear of their soul being stolen. More experienced Rootworkers use dolls for this purpose and, as in Vodun, they "baptize" and consecrate the doll to be whomever they wish. The dolls are traditionally made out of handsewn cloth and stuffed with Spanish moss or herbs, but today many Rootworkers find it easier to purchase one from a toy store. Another method was taking the earth left by a person's footprint. This is a direct extension of the West African belief that a person's energy can be captured in the tracks they leave behind. This method is rarely used except in the very rural parts of the South where roads are not yet paved with cement.

SPIRITS OF THE DEAD

IN THE PAST FEW YEARS there has been a renewed interest in spiritual guides and a host of books on their function in our lives. However, very few give a clear, down-to-earth explanation on who they are, what they are, and how they work. Unfortunately, most people group all spirits into one lovely, cheery, smiling category, but this is a mistake. What are spirits? Are they winged beings bearing a message of love, compassion, and the greater good? Sure, some of them are, but they are simply the spirits of dead *people.* I emphasize the word *people* because most of us think that just because Aunt Jane passed on that she no longer has the prejudices and preferences she had when she had a physical body. Enlightenment takes work, and just because we pass to the other side doesn't mean we automatically become wise. According to Hoodoo tradition there are four types of spirits.

Highly Elevated—

These are the souls of the righteous who reached an extremely high level of spiritual growth when they were alive. They are incorruptible, and cannot be used to do any negative spiritual work or black magic. Their sole purpose is one of service, to protect and guide the living.

Ancestors—

These are the souls of your deceased family members. Their role is difficult to define because that depends on how you interacted with them in life. Most of the ancestors that walk with you probably died long before you were born, but it is important to talk to them about your feelings, how they can help you with problems, family affairs, etc. They usually work extremely fast to get results if you take care of them with regular prayers and offerings.

Spiritual Guides—

These are the souls of people related or unrelated that have chosen to help you, either for their own spiritual growth, yours, or both. It's similar to a work study program in the spiritual world. I must reiterate that just because a spirit wants to communicate with you doesn't mean you have to. Use the same discretion with them as you would with any living person before they gain your absolute trust. Trust is gained from accurate advice and results. Use your good common sense with spiritual guides just as you would with living people. Note that spiritual guides can be of *any* age, race, or religion and the same goes for your ancestors or your guardian angel.

Misguided or Dark Spirits—

These are the souls of people who died unhappy, led unhappy lives, or were just negative in life. Contrary to popular belief, most misguided or dark spirits do not intentionally try to hurt people (though some do). You can easily spot them because they may offer an inappropriate solution or one that will create more trouble than the problem you started out with. They are only giving you advice based on their own negative experiences. Some troubled spirits may be upset that they no longer have a body and create inappropriate bonds with the living. Sometimes they will become attached to a person and try to bring them to the other side. This may be because they miss a living person and want to be reunited with them, or because someone they care about is unhappy on this plane and they are trying to put them out of their misery. In rare cases a really misguided spirit will attach itself to someone just to wreak havoc. Traditionally, these spirits are the cause of freak accidents and bad luck.

HOW DO I COMMUNICATE WITH THEM?

There are several ways to communicate with spirits. The ability to communicate with them is mainly an extension of your ability to listen. All you have to do is learn how to quiet your logical mind by not questioning everything and allow your intuitive faculty to take over for a change. This takes time to develop but once they know you're trying, they won't stop communicating with you and you may have to tell them to shut up! Many people strengthen this ability through learning some form of divination such as the Tarot. Your guides work through these tools to communicate with you until you are skilled enough to hear them clearly without it. Rootworkers try as much as possible to strengthen this skill by simply sitting in front of a person and relaying the information that comes to them from their spiritual guides. This is not to diminish the use of divinatory tools, but it is important not to depend on them. If you're in a crisis situation, there won't be time to do a card spread. Try reading for your friends or family with just a glass of water and a candle every now and then. Here's how:

Step 1—Wait until you're alone or won't be interrupted.

Step 2—Make sure you and your client are in a calm state of mind. It's never a good idea to do a reading for someone when you or they are extremely emotional or intoxicated because neither of you would be able to focus enough to give or absorb the information.

Step 3—Before you begin, say a prayer for yourself and your
clients, asking the ancestors and spiritual guides to
assist in making the reading as enlightening as possible. Ask your client to name a few of their relatives
that have passed on either aloud or to themselves,
and you should do the same. Light a votive candle in
their honor. It should burn out by the end of the
session.

Step 4—Take a glass of regular tap water and place it beside
the candle to symbolize purity and clarity.

If you practice, you'll begin to see astonishing results. It may
start out with seeing objects or hearing a word. Whatever it is,
don't ignore it. Say whatever comes to you and let the other person make sense of it. If nothing resonates with the client you
must be firm with your guides to be more specific or ask your
client to think harder. Please don't feel silly or embarrassed by
whatever you're hearing or seeing because something that may
seem ridiculous to you may hold real meaning for your client. I
must also mention that once your guides realize you really trust
them they will continue to give you information.

HOW DO I HONOR THEM?

Since the beginning of time and in all cultures, people have hon-
ored their ancestors with elaborate rituals and offerings based on the

belief in the continuity of life. Deceased relatives were not seen as nonexistent but as having changed form, like water to steam. Although they no longer had a physical body their soul lived on, and to ancient people the soul was the animating force of life, not the mind or the heart. It is with this understanding that the ancients realized that the ancestors could still affect the lives of the living for good or ill long after physical death. That is why these societies thought it would be in their best interest to give offerings to their ancestors to ensure their blessing and assistance in everyday matters. Although this belief has died out for many in the West and other "modern" nations, there are still others around the world who have maintained the old ways. By honoring those who came before us and including them in our everyday lives, we will benefit from their wisdom and gain a much-needed helping hand. Many will also realize that they no longer have the fear of old age and death that plague many Westernized people.

One way to honor your ancestors is to create an ancestral altar. There are really no set rules for how to create one except that it should be clean and well maintained. Set aside private space on a table or other surface for you to burn candles or place offerings or other implements so you can communicate with your guides. Traditionally, a glass or glasses of water are placed there for any thirsty visitors, along with rum for those who liked to drink. A white cloth is commonly used to cover the table, but feel free to improvise. Some people will go on and on about the proper way to create an altar, but how you decorate it is completely up to you and your guides. Out of respect don't have sex near or around your altar.

Here are a few more ways to honor your heritage in a less formal way:

1. Observe Kwanzaa or any other traditional holidays that celebrate whoever your ethnic group were *prior* to slavery or colonization.

2. Keep a white candle lit while you are awake for the millions of Africans that died during Maafa (the Middle Passage) and all the ones that survived. Never forget we are the descendants of the strongest, the ones that *made it.*

3. Read books on Black history to get a better understanding of who we are and who we were.

4. Take a day off work for the birthday of the black hero or heroine of your choice. Just because Malcolm X, Huey Newton, Harriet Tubman, and Sojourner Truth don't have a national holiday doesn't mean we can't celebrate them by making our own.

5. Implement cultural elements into wedding services and births.

6. Respect, honor, and appreciate your family.

DIVINITORY METHODS
OF ROOTWORKERS

DIVINATION IS VERY IMPORTANT to Rootworkers, as they are relied on by clients to perform some kind of oracular function on their behalf in addition to spell work. However, Rootdoctors never do fortune telling the way it is known today. Only charlatans claim to know the future. Instead, Rootworkers work in the realm of possibility because it is considered arrogant to think you can see God's plan. What an oracle does is tell you the *likely* outcome of events as they exist at the moment of the reading unless something is done to change it. However, some mainstream religions consider the use of spells as interfering with another person's free will. True Rootworkers understand that free will is God given and no one can negate it. That which is truly yours could never be taken away. Divination allows us to know the forces at work that are guiding our lives and whatever problem we came to the Rootworker to resolve. Here are just a few of the divination methods most commonly used:

Aeromancy:

Divining the future by studying aerial phenomena such as cloud formations and wind currents.

Alectromancy:

Observing the flight patterns and the order of pecking birds to gain insight into the future.

Apantomancy:

An omen interpreted by the sudden appearance of a wild animal that is rarely seen otherwise. Seeing a buzzard was considered to be a certain sign that someone was about to die.

Astagalomancy:

Throwing sticks, dice, bones, or rocks on a table or on the ground to divine the future. A respectable example of this practice can be seen in the movie *The Autobiography of Miss Jane Pittman.*

Astrology:

System based on the belief that the positions of the stars and planets affect a person's destiny. Traditionally, Rootworkers only paid attention to the phases of the moon to plan the best time to do certain spells. Today we have access to charts and astrological calendars for maximum efficiency for the proper timing of spells. Here I have listed the phases of the moon and how they can be worked with:

- **New**—This phase is a great time to begin new projects, break bad habits, or get rid of any beliefs or people that are holding you back.

- **Waxing**—As the moon grows fuller so does its powerful spiritual energies. The seeds you planted during the new moon are now in a gestation period.

- **Full**—The moon is at its peak of power at this time. It is a great time to internalize affirmations or perform rituals or any other spiritual activity. Forgive yourself for any mistakes you have made and let them melt away with the waning moon.

- **Waning**—During this phase reflect on your goals and accomplishments. If you have not seen the fruits of your labor yet, don't worry. Another new moon is right around the corner.

Bibliomancy:
Flipping to a random page in the Bible and pointing to a random place on the page to answer a question.

Cartomancy:

Divination by using cards. Traditionally playing cards were used but now there are a myriad of Tarot decks on the market for Rootworkers to explore. I recommend The New Orleans Voodoo Tarot, Romani Tarot, and Tarot of the Orishas. Playing cards are just as effective and were used to great efficacy by Rootworkers in the past and present. The first step is to buy a separate deck of cards that are different from the ones used for games. It is important to treat the deck with respect as a spiritual tool. It is advised that you keep them wrapped in a nice cloth or scarf and in a safe place when not in use. If you plan to read cards, you must never gamble with cards again. It is considered taboo to exploit the deck for these purposes. Before conducting a reading, I would advise that you follow the same steps and suggestions I outlined in the spirit communication section.

Hearts

The suit of hearts represents the emotional life, dreams, love, creativity, domestic issues, and spiritual matters associated with earthly pleasure. It is for this reason that hearts are considered the most fortunate in the deck. Water element.

• **Ace of hearts**—Happiness and spiritual blessings.

- **Queen of hearts**—A passionate and spiritual woman who puts her ideals into practice. She is creative and powerful. If this card indicates a man, he is the sensitive type.

- **King of hearts**—A generous, affectionate man with a heart of gold. If this card indicates a woman, she is emotionally stable and independent.

- **Jack of hearts**—A kind friend that you have or will meet. If this card indicates a woman, she is far from shy and will speak her mind without apology.

- **Two of hearts**—Abundance and prosperity is indicated. A special partnership, attraction, and commitment.

- **Three of hearts**—A time for celebration. Happiness and friendship. When surrounded by spades, it could indicate deceit by someone close to you.

- **Four of hearts**—Discontent with life. Delays, disappointments, and broken promises. After the party, the dawn brings reality.

- **Five of hearts**—Extremely lucky card. Spiritual seekers and those with higher knowledge are indicated.

- **Six of hearts**—Unexpected good fortune. May also indicate a person that doesn't appreciate what they have. Count your blessings and expect more out of life.

- **Seven of hearts**—A card of illusions and delusions of grandeur. If surrounded by positive cards, it can indicate a reunion with an old friend.

- **Eight of hearts**—This card indicates a change in attitude or re-evaluation of the matter at hand. You may receive an invitation to a party if the three of hearts is in the same spread.

- **Nine of hearts**—The wish card. This card indicates emotional fulfillment of desires.

- **Ten of hearts**—Good fortune and happiness. A combination of all the fortunate cards in the suit. Don't worry about a thing.

Spades

The suit of swords represents mental and spiritual development, obstacles, treachery, and loss. They caution the reader on the perils ahead and how they can be avoided through clear and rational thinking. Air element.

• **Ace of spades**—The death card that indicates the end or completion of something. It could be either negative or positive depending on the surrounding cards.

• **Queen of spades**—An aggressive, intelligent, and proud woman. If this card indicates a man, he has the same qualities but he is sneakier, a wolf in sheep's clothing.

• **King of spades**—An egotistical, macho, morally devoid man. If this card represents a woman, she can never be trusted.

• **Jack of spades**—A solemn, introverted man with problems expressing his feelings. If this card indicates a female, the meaning is the same.

• **Two of spades**—Indecisiveness, scandal, laziness.

• **Three of spades**—Sorrow, adultery, poor judgment.

• **Four of spades**—Bitterness, a separation from a mate, failure, illness. A person that works too hard.

• **Five of spades**—Self-pity, depression, and anxiety are indicated. Things will get better but you must change the things you know are holding you back.

- **Six of spades**—Things are improving but you must not get lazy. Keep fighting and all will turn out in your favor. Struggle a bit longer, there's a light at the end of the tunnel.

- **Seven of spades**—Careful planning before taking a risk. It could work if you don't jump in head-first. If surrounded by other negative cards, it isn't a good move at all.

- **Eight of spades**—Self-empowerment and growth is indicated when surrounded by positive cards. Loss and trouble if surrounded by negative cards.

- **Nine of spades**—The card of drastic change or flash of inspiration. The change cannot be avoided whether for positive or negative, so just go with the flow. The more you fight it the worse it will get. This card has a bad reputation ever since Dorothy Dandridge pulled it in *Carmen Jones*, depicting her demise.

- **Ten of spades**—It's been a long, tough road but the sun peeks out from the storm clouds. You will see improvement shortly.

♣Clubs

Enterprise, entreupreneurship, creative integrity, inner development, business, and loyalty. Fire element.

- **Ace of clubs**—Achievement of goals, change, and success. Finally getting your due.

- **Queen of clubs**—A confident, intelligent woman with considerable occult knowledge or capabilities. If this card represents a man, he may be somewhat eccentric.

- **King of clubs**—An honest man that plays fair and works hard. If this card represents a woman, she is probably tough as nails with piercing eyes that seem to look right through you.

- **Jack of clubs**—A confident, passionate man with strong beliefs and high values. Has the world all figured out. If this indicates a woman, the meaning is intensified. She can be dominating and has to get the last word in an argument.

- **Two of clubs**—Laziness or delays completing a task already started. Procrastination.

- **Three of clubs**—Hard work is payed off. May indicate a raise, promotion, or the success of a creative effort.

- **Four of clubs**—Things are moving slowly but it's for the best. Clarity is needed for the querist to get what they want. An indication that someone might be misinformed and trouble may be the result of ignorance.

- **Five of clubs**—A period of struggle. Financial or health problems.

- **Six of clubs**—This card indicates business success and a relief from financial difficulties after a long period of struggle. Triumph.

- **Seven of clubs**—Re-evaluation. Things are not going as well as you planned. Use a new plan of action to succeed in the long run. All is not lost but you won't make it if you're not strong or persistent.

- **Eight of clubs**—The horse with blinders card. Make sure you stay focused on the goal you set for yourself. This card indicates distractions, especially from the opposite sex. Don't let anyone get in the way or the crop you planted may wilt and die before it has a chance to sprout.

- **Nine of clubs**—The finish line is approaching. Your goals are almost in sight after a lot of hard work. Triumph after a final challenge.

- **Ten of clubs**—Good fortune and completion. A surprise is just around the corner; unexpected money perhaps?

Diamonds

Craftmanship, generosity, finances, stability, health. Earth element.

- **Ace of diamonds**—An unexpected boon. Money, an engagement ring, or any gifts are indicated. Excellent chances at winning at gambling. Take a trip to the casino!

- **Queen of diamonds**—A materialistic woman with a strong head for business. Very kind and resourceful. If this card represents a man, the characteristics are the same but he could be envious of others.

- **King of diamonds**—An intense, stubborn man but generally a good person. If this card represents a woman, she is a genuine, trustworthy friend and confidante.

- **Jack of diamonds**—A goal-oriented man with a strong disposition. If this card represents a woman, she is creative and friendly.

- **Two of diamonds**—A positive change after being broke or ill.

- **Three of diamonds**—Successful outcome. Monetary reward and career glory.

- **Four of diamonds**—Life is improving but your doubts are getting in the way. If you stop being pessimistic, things will go much smoother. Low self-esteem and depression.

- **Five of diamonds**—This is an extremely auspicious card. The wheel of fortune tilts in your favor. Make the most of this lucky time!

- **Six of diamonds**—Life is hectic and demanding. Try to keep up with things and don't give up, you'll be glad you did. Usually comes up for artists or other creative-minded people.

- **Seven of diamonds**—Things are going a bit smoother

than they were but it's not party time just yet. There is still a lot of work to do and if you get lazy all will be lost. Don't be so smug!

- **Eight of diamonds**—Take a chance. The universe will be on your side.

- **Nine of diamonds**—Opportunities for financial and career growth abound. Take advantage of the doors that fling open even if you think you can't. An unexpected pleasant surprise will come soon.

- **Ten of diamonds**—The luckiest card in the suit. It promises all the good things that life has to offer. Wipe your tears and prepare for lots of laughter and fun. If you are unemployed, you will find a job soon.

Lychnomancy:

Divination by candles. Interpreting how they burn, smoke patterns, and deciphering shapes from the wax to determine whether a wish will come true.

Remote viewing:

Ability to see the events in another place from a distance. This ability was depicted in the wonderful movie *Eve's Bayou.*

Scrying:

Gazing at the surface of any smooth or polished surface to obtain messages about the future. Rootworkers cracked an egg in a bowl of water and deciphered the swirling patterns it created.

Stolisomancy:

Using the way a person dresses to figure them out. Some Rootworkers demanded that their clients wear white and a head tie so they wouldn't be accused of this less-respected form of divination.

UNDERSTANDING SPELLS FOR LOVE, MONEY, AND SUCCESS

UNDERSTANDING SPELLS FOR
LOVE, MONEY, AND SUCCESS

MANY OF THE SPELLS in this book are traditional Rootwork spells that have been adapted for your convenience and are just as effective. This is because some of the ingredients commonly used in the old spells simply aren't easily available these days, especially in large cities (unless you know someone who might have a possum's tail lying around). Rootwork survived the perilous voyage to America because of its ability to adapt. In order for it to survive into the twenty-first century, it is essential to tailor information for the modern reader.

You will also notice that many of the ingredients for these spells are easy to attain or already in your pantry in keeping with the traditional Rootwork belief in making things simple. Many contemporary spell books have a laundry list of expensive, mass-produced ingredients (that are, I must admit, fun to use) leaving you more broke than when you started. Rootworkers pride themselves on being practical and truly believe that less is more.

That said, we can talk about adapting spells. I welcome you to be as creative as you want to be, just be careful not to change the general order of the steps. As I've mentioned many times before, it is important to personalize any magickal spell. If you get the notion to use some other ingredient, flower, or color candle in place of the one suggested, by all means do so. Please don't think you're doing something wrong, just go with your gut and you can't go wrong. Good Luck!

BEFORE YOU BEGIN

To get the most out of this book I have a few tips to give you before you get started.

1. Use Common Sense

Perform spells for the things you need first and the things you want later.

For example, a young man came to a Rootworker because he wanted to date a beautiful lady that lived across the street who consistently ignored him. He wanted a spell to get her to notice and go out with him. The Rootworker asked the man why he didn't want a spell to find a job since he was unemployed, but he insisted that he'd worry about that later. It wasn't her place to argue with a client so she gave him what he wanted, and within two weeks and three days' time he and the beautiful lady were dating. It didn't take long before his lack of money and inability to take the lady out became a real issue in their relationship. He came back to her depressed and wanted a spell to keep her with him. That's when the Rootworker drew the line and told him that he needed to focus on solving the root of the problem, finding a decent job. If she hadn't put her foot down, he would've come back every week for something else.

2. Intention

Always be clear on your reasons for performing a spell. Ask yourself if it is in your best interest to have whatever you are asking for and why. If after careful examination, you realize you really don't want whatever you're seeking or it just doesn't feel right, let it go.

3. Remain Focused

It is extremely important when doing any spell to remain focused. Scattered thoughts are sure to produce undesirable results if you don't approach things with a clear head. That is why it is suggested not to use any mind-altering drugs or alcohol when doing a spell. If you live with other people ask them politely not to interrupt you, or you can simply wait till they're not home or asleep.

TAYANNAH LEE MCQUILLAR

4. Have Patience and Forget About It

The greatest "spell-killer" is obsession and impatience. Try not to think about it anymore once it's done. Remember, you are not David Copperfield and nothing will "poof" as soon as you've completed your spell. All things come in good time.

SPELLS FOR LOVE

"CLEOPATRA" SPELL TO ATTRACT A PARTICULAR MAN

WRITE THE NAME of the man you want nine times on a piece of brown paper bag. Write your name over his in pencil (the color of the lead doesn't matter) and fold the paper toward you five times. If he is a black or dark-complexioned man, put the paper in a bottle of thick dark syrup. If he's white or light-complexioned, place in a bottle of light syrup.

"MACK DADDY" SPELL TO GET A WOMAN'S INTEREST

THIS SPELL WORKS ESPECIALLY well on women who are cold, shy, or distant. Take a purple candle and write her name with a needle (or any sharp instrument) three times on it coming toward you. Anoint the candle with rose, magnet, or Come to Me oil. (You can buy these oils from your local metaphysical store or see my resources section.) Sprinkle some table salt on it and burn it right away. You'll see a noticeable change within a few days.

"DIVINE RETRIBUTION" SPELL TO GET BACK AT A WOMAN THAT'S DONE YOU WRONG

GET A BLUE SEVEN-DAY candle and dedicate it to St. Christopher. Tell him what the woman did to break your heart and he'll make sure she pays for it. According to legend, St. Christopher was a eunuch who didn't care for women. Burn the candle completely and leave the empty glass in front of a church at night.

"SCORNED WOMAN" SPELL TO GET BACK AT A MAN THAT'S DONE YOU WRONG

THIS IS AN EXTREMELY POTENT spell not to be performed if there is any chance of reconciliation.

Take raw beef chunks (as you would use to make stew) or steak and think about how the man hurt you. Carry the meat to a place where you know a big dog is located and taunt the dog with the meat till it gets mad (make sure it's chained up or behind a fence). Spit on the meat and say the man's name before you throw the meat at the angry dog to devour, then walk away.

SPELL TO GET SOMEONE YOU'RE INTERESTED IN TO VISIT YOUR HOME

USE A THICK PINK CANDLE if the person is a woman or a red candle if the person is a man. Write their name on the candle with a sharp instrument three times, then take four straight pins and stick them deep into the candle in the form of a cross. Burn for one hour twice a day until it's gone. Once the candle is burned out take a little of the leftover wax and sprinkle it on the path leading to your home. Invite the person over after five days and they'll come even if they had no previous intention of doing so.

"STUCK ON YOU" SPELL TO ATTRACT A PARTICULAR WOMAN

TAKE ANY KIND OF WRAPPED CANDY and rub it on the bottom of your feet. Whisper your desires to the candy and give it to her. She won't know why, but she'll start being attracted to you.

"TRUE TO ME" SPELL TO KEEP A MAN FAITHFUL

This is a powerful spell from New Orleans. You may use any symbol of your religious faith instead of a cross as long as it represents truth and justice.

Take a condom full of the man's sperm and tie it in a knot. Wrap it around a cross with the image of the crucified Jesus on the front. Dip the cross into holy water from a Catholic church. Place it under the bed or in a secret place in a closet both of you share. If he tries to cheat the guilt will eat him alive and make him stop.

"HELPING HAND" SPELL TO SEPARATE A COUPLE

YOU MUST BE EITHER single or in a good relationship to perform this spell or you'll break up your own.

Write the names of the two people you want to break up on opposite sides of a single piece of paper nine times. Rip the paper violently in half and cry for their relationship. Wipe the water from your tears across both their names and place the paper under a white candle dedicated to St. Rita. Burn the candle until it goes out. According to legend, St. Rita was in an abusive relationship and will break up any abusive relationship if you ask her to. This spell is especially powerful for this purpose. *Do not* use this spell simply to get a man you want.

"HOMEWRECKER" SPELL TO CAUSE SERIOUS DISCORD IN THE HOME OF A LOVER LIVING WITH SOMEONE ELSE

MIX A HALF CUP EACH of black pepper, red pepper, goofer dust, and leaves from a dead pink rose.

Grind the ingredients into a fine powder. Put the powder into a plastic bag, fill it with cigar smoke, and close it, being careful to seal in the smoke. Sprinkle around their door or apartment building when no one is around.

"THROUGH WITH YOU" SPELL TO MAKE A MAN LEAVE YOU ALONE

ONLY USE THIS SPELL if you're absolutely sure you don't want this man in your life.

Mix together a half cup of graveyard dirt from a road leading out of the cemetery, a half cup of red pepper, and a tablespoon of salt. Think about whatever the man did to make you mad, then throw the mixture in front of his workplace or apartment. This will bring trouble to the man until he leaves you alone.

"ALWAYS ON MY MIND" SPELL TO MAKE A MAN THINK ABOUT YOU

TAKE A PICTURE of your lover and place it on the back of your headboard upside down. Make sure the picture of him faces the headboard, as if it were looking at you through the headboard as you sleep. This will make your lover think about you.

"LEASH ON YOU" SPELL TO BRING HIM BACK

TAKE A GLASS OF WATER and put a picture of your lover in it upside down. Make sure the picture is big enough to stand up in the glass. If the picture is small, use a shot glass. Put the glass near the bed. Light a white candle next to it to guide him back to you.

"SAY YOU'RE SORRY" SPELL TO MAKE SOMEONE CALM DOWN AFTER AN ARGUMENT

WRITE THE NAME of the angry person five times on a piece of paper, place it in a plastic container full of water, and put it in the freezer. This will cool the person down considerably and often makes them apologize. You can leave the container in the freezer if you want to prevent future confrontations.

"CHEAPER TO KEEP HER" SPELL TO KEEP A WIFE FAITHFUL

TAKE A RED SEVEN-DAY candle and tie the woman's panties around it in as many knots as you can, each time saying, "You belong to me." Cut a little of your pubic hair and sprinkle it inside the candle, and say her name right before you light it. After letting the candle burn all the way down, wrap the panties around something heavy like a small lead pipe or hammer. This is a phallic symbol to keep her right where you want her. Hide it where she won't find it.

"STAY PUT!" SPELL TO
KEEP A MAN WITH YOU

CUT A SQUARE from the center of the man's unwashed underwear. Take hair from his comb and his fingernail clippings. Place them all in a jar. Scrape the bottom of a pair of shoes he wears often and place the residue in the jar (the amount doesn't matter). Urinate in the jar and seal it tightly. Hide it in a place where he won't find it.

"GOING TO THE CHAPEL" SPELL TO MAKE YOUR LOVER MARRY YOU

THIS SPELL IS TO BE DONE at night and should only be performed by someone already in a relationship.

Make a list of all the things distracting your lover from wanting to commit to you. Burn a black candle over the list for nine days. On the night of the ninth day go to a cemetery and bury the list over any grave that you seem attracted to. Write down the name on the headstone (in a notebook or someplace else you won't lose it) and ask the spirit of the person buried there to help you get what you want. Pay the spirit with nine pennies, fruit, or white flowers. The next day run yourself a lukewarm bath with a half cup of Florida Water and the petals of any kind of yellow flower. Make sure that your body is clean *before* you get in; this bath is just to soak, not to wash in. Meditate on why you and your lover should get married. After you're done, take a cup or a jar and put a little of the bath water in it. Sprinkle it in front of your home or apartment door and around the bedroom.

Light a white candle dedicated to the spirit of the grave, asking him/her to persuade your partner to marry you. Let the candle burn completely. Tell him/her to put strong signs and messages in your lover's path to show them that marrying you is the right thing for them to do. You will get what you want.

"ALL NIGHT LONG" SPELL TO IMPROVE YOUR SEX LIFE

WIPE YOUR GENITALS with a new handkerchief or scarf (any color or material will do), then wipe your lover's genitals with it. Put it in a jar with red hot peppers saturated with honey. Things are sure to heat up.

"THREE'S A CROWD" SPELL TO MAKE YOUR LOVER'S EX BACK OFF

BUY A DOLL or teddy bear with a soft body and name it after the person annoying you. Using a knife or scissors, rip the stuffing out of the stomach. Whisper in the doll's ear that is what will happen if they continue to harass your lover. Blind the doll with duct tape and take it to a street running the opposite way of the street outside your home. Throw it in front of oncoming traffic and don't look back.

"MIGHTY LOVE" SPELL TO FIND YOUR SOUL MATE

LIGHT TWO WHITE seven-day candles, one for your guardian angel and the other for your soul mate's. Pray to both of your guardian angels to find a way to bring you together wherever he or she may be. (You must not have *any* preconceived notions of what he or she looks like or anything else about them, because it would make the spell superficial. Your soul mate might not look like Denzel Washington or Brad Pitt, but he or she will make you happy.) Tie the candles together with a pretty pink satin ribbon and make a bow. Once the candles have burned out, place the empty glasses with the ribbon still around them in a plastic bag. Place it in front of a church or any place you feel is holy.

"THRILL IS GONE" SPELL TO MAKE A WOMAN LEAVE YOU ALONE

TAKE A PAIR of her panties and cut them into tiny pieces. Place the pieces in a bottle (any kind will do) with a lid and toss it over your shoulder into a river, the ocean, or any running water. Don't look back.

"BOW DOWN BOY" SPELL TO MAKE A MAN DO WHAT YOU WANT

THIS IS A POTENT SPELL of domination, excellent for use on a stubborn, headstrong mate.

This spell is to be done while you're on your menstrual cycle. Buy a black seven-day candle and a white skull candle (purchase at your local metaphysical store or see the resources section at the back of this book). Carve your initials into the eye sockets of the skull candle and on the forehead. Write your mate's name and birthdate above the head. Next, write your name and birthdate directly above his. Take some of your menstrual blood and make the sign of the cross (or star of David, pentagram, etc.) on top of the birthdates. After that, take a knife and scrape the wax from the mouth until it's smooth. *There should be nothing left where the mouth was.* Lightly dab the wick of the black candle in some more menstrual blood and light it. Light the wick of the skull candle from the flame of the black candle. Burn until the candles are gone.

SPELLS FOR MONEY

"FULL REGISTER" SPELL TO INCREASE BUSINESS

TAKE A PAIL (any kind will do) of water, add five teaspoons of honey, two magnets, and five drops of Come to Me or Attraction oil (see resources section). Let it sit for a few hours. Take out the magnets and throw the water in front of your business late at night or when no one is around. Do this during every new moon.

"SWEET SUCCESS" SPELL TO
KEEP CUSTOMERS COMING BACK

KEEP A BOWL ANOINTED with bayberry oil filled with candies by the cash register. This will encourage customers to come back and to tell other people about your business. If you keep a mailing list of customers, anoint the corners every couple of weeks with Money Drawing oil.

"EASY BOSS" SPELL TO GET A RAISE OR PROMOTION

WRITE DOWN THE NAMES of your boss (any color pencil will do) and all the people that can influence your job on a piece of brown paper bag. Take a jar of honey and spill half of it on grass close to your home. Submerge the list in the rest of the honey, urinate in the jar until full, and sprinkle controlling powder (see resources) in it. Your bosses will be eating out of your hands.

"FOR THE LOVE OF MONEY" SPELL TO WIN AT GAMBLING

TAKE A DOLLAR BILL, roll it up into a cylinder, and tie it with a red piece of thread. Make nine knots in the thread, making sure you breathe the word *luck* in each knot before tightly securing it. Make a liar kiss it and dress it with Money Drawing oil (five drops) before you play. Keep it in your pocket.

"AIN'T TOO PROUD TO BEG"
SPELL TO SUCCESSFULLY WRITE
A LETTER ASKING FOR MONEY

RUB THE PAPER (any kind of paper) with cornmeal and a fresh sprig of parsley. Write your letter in pen or pencil. Turn down the edges on all four corners. Pray out loud for what you need and seal in an envelope.

"HIGH JOHN THE CONQUEROR" SPELL TO ATTRACT MONEY

What you'll need:

five walnuts in the shell
ten pumpkin seeds (unsalted)
One piece of High John the Conqueror root
A single pink or yellow rose
Your favorite perfume or cologne

BOIL THE WALNUTS, pumpkin seeds, and High John the Conqueror root until the water turns a dark brown. Strain the mixture and put it in a jar to cool. Draw yourself a warm bath and pour the contents of the jar in the water. Add the petals of the pink or yellow rose along with the perfume or cologne. Focus on drawing money to you and try not to worry about where it's going to come from. Try to avoid distractions, enjoy your bath (for at least fifteen minutes) and relax. Do this for five consecutive days (or nights).

"BIG BANK BOOK" CANDLE SPELL TO ATTRACT MONEY

THIS IS A VERY POWERFUL candle dressing to attract money. In a bowl or saucer, mix a tablespoon of honey and a teaspoon of sugar until it makes a thick paste. Apply lightly on a green candle. If you are using a seven-day candle, just smear a light layer on the wax around the wick. Dust lightly with cinnamon powder. Before you light the candle, take a little honey from the bowl and dab it on your tongue and tell the candle what you want it to do. Enjoy the sweetness of the honey, light the candle, and pray that the outcome of the spell will be just as sweet.

"YOU'RE HIRED!"

SPELL TO FIND A JOB

WEAR A PAIR OF OLD SHOES that you're willing to throw away and go to a park or forest. Bring along a brown candle, any kind of fruit, and also bring a new pair of shoes. Go to a secluded area and pray for stability, opportunities, and a great job. Place the candle and fruit against a healthy-looking tree, light the candle, and leave them there. Take off your old shoes and leave them against the tree, put on the new shoes, and as you're leaving pick up a few stones or rocks in your path. Make sure you exit the park or forest using a different route. When you get home, place the rocks on top of your resume or carry them when you look for work.

"PAY ME NOW!" SPELL TO GET BACK MONEY OWED TO YOU

TAP YOUR MAILBOX five times with a picture of or personal object belonging to the person that owes you money. Take that same picture or object and put it behind your toilet. The person will lose things until they pay you back.

"HARD TIMES" SPELL TO GET SOMEONE TO LOAN YOU MONEY

LIGHT A YELLOW CANDLE dedicated to Saint Caridad del Cobre (no statue necessary) for five days, asking her to bring out the person's generosity and kindness to you. You will get the money you need.

SPELLS FOR SUCCESS

"SAINT EXPEDITE" SPELL
FOR EMERGENCY LUCK

THIS IS A traditional spell from New Orleans.

Take a small red candle dedicated to Saint Expedite(no statue necessary) and burn it on a Monday, Wednesday, or Friday until it burns out completely. Pray for what you need and he will act quickly. Always give him an offering of cake or fruit once your wish has been granted. You may leave the offering on your altar for seven days or leave it in front of a church after three days.

"EVERYTHING MY WAY"
SPELL TO INCREASE LUCK

GET A HORSESHOE and some gold and silver glitter. Add glue to the tips of both ends of the horseshoe and dip one end in gold and the other in silver. Hang it above your front door with the ends facing up.

"HIGHER CONSCIOUSNESS"
SPELL FOR PEACE AND CLARITY

PUT EIGHT COTTON BALLS in your mouth and speak out loud about everything that is troubling you. If you feel the need to cry, do it. After you're finished remove the cotton balls and put them aside. Run yourself a cool bath and add a cup of coconut milk and three sprigs of fresh basil. Immerse yourself in the water for at least twenty minutes. Dress in clean, white or light-colored clothing and light three small white candles. One is for peace, the other for clarity, and the third for your soul. Discard the cotton balls any way you see fit.

"REBIRTH" SPELL TO RELEASE NEGATIVITY AND CREATE CHANGE

THIS SPELL IS EXTREMELY potent. Make sure you are ready for dramatic change before undertaking it. This spell will remove anything or anyone in your life that doesn't belong or is holding you back. Expect the unexpected.

The night before you perform this spell, sleep in old clothes that can be thrown away. In the first hours of dawn the following morning, rip the clothes off your body aggressively and put them in a plastic bag. Light a black seven-day candle and pray for all negative influences in your life to disappear. Make sure the candle burns out completely. Take the bag and an eggplant to the gate of a cemetery and leave them there. Try not to fight the changes once they begin to manifest.

"HEALTHY AS A HORSE" SPELL TO IMPROVE AND MAINTAIN HEALTH

MIX A HALF CUP of Florida Water perfume, a half cup of rose water, seeds from six red apples, and petals from any red flower in a lukewarm bath. Soak for at least a half hour while visualizing yourself in optimum health. Burn an orange seven-day candle until it's gone.

"MOTHER-TO-BE"
SPELL FOR FERTILITY

SHAKE THE LEFT HAND of a pregnant woman with your right hand, then rub her stomach three times. Eat fish for dinner for three days afterward (including the day you touch the pregnant woman). Pray to the spirit of your unborn child for help and light a white candle in their honor until it burns out.

"UPROOT ME"
MOJO BAG FOR CHANGE

IN A RED FLANNEL BAG combine the dirt from around a fire department, a butcher shop, a police station, and a high school. Include a semiprecious cat's-eye stone and tie it up. Wear the bag against your skin.

"CONSTANT INSPIRATION"
SPELL FOR CREATIVITY

PLACE A LAPIS LAZULI or cat's-eye stone under your pillow at night and you'll never run out of ideas.

"MAGICK MIRROR"
SPELL FOR PROTECTION

PLACE A SMALL MIRROR behind the door of your bedroom with the back facing outside. Negativity will be reflected back to whomever sends it.

"REDEEM ME"
SPELL FOR FORGIVENESS

TAKE THE WHITES from eight eggs and put them in a bowl. Pour the egg whites into a tub of lukewarm water and soak for about an hour as you pray for forgiveness. Egg whites are excellent removers of negative energy. Light a white candle for clarity until it burns out.

THE FOLLOWING RECIPES are for mojo bags. See the "Talismans and Charms" section on page 31 for full instructions.

"BLESSED LADY"
MOJO FOR GENERAL LUCK

What you'll need:

1 rabbit's foot
A lock of your hair
3 fingernail clippings
1/2 teaspoon mustard seeds
1 lodestone
1 wishbone
5 alfalfa sprouts

"MR. RIGHT" MOJO TO ATTRACT A LOVER

What you'll need:

- 5 pomegranate seeds
- A small key
- 1 orrisroot
- 5 strands of pubic hair
- 1 moonstone

"THIRD EYE" MOJO FOR PSYCHIC ABILITY

What you'll need:

A lock of hair from a black cat
13 anise seeds
1/2 teaspoon cemetery dirt
7 fish scales
A lock of hair from the back of your head
1/2 teaspoon sea salt
1 obsidian stone

"KING MIDAS"
MOJO FOR LUCK

What you'll need:

- 1 teaspoon gold glitter
- 3 fingernail clippings
- 1 lodestone
- 1 High John the Conqueror root
- 1 copper penny

"BINGO" MOJO FOR GAMBLING

What you'll need:

- 1 tonka bean
- 2 green dice
- 6 apple seeds
- 1 dollar bill
- A picture of Saint Expedite

"RUN DEVIL"
MOJO FOR PROTECTION

What you'll need:

- 1 tiger's-eye stone (semiprecious)
- 1 tiny cross
- 10 dried crushed basil leaves
- 1 teaspoon church earth
- A lock of your hair
- 1 white feather
- A small metal nail

"ONE NIGHT STAND"
MOJO FOR QUICK SEX

What you'll need:

    A clipping of hair from your armpit
    A clipping of pubic hair
    toenail clippings
    1 teaspoon Vervain
    6 cloves
    1 cinnamon stick
    2 magnets

"PO' NO MO"
MOJO FOR MONEY

What you'll need:

1 tonka bean
1 rabbit's foot
1 High John the Conqueror root
1 Lodestone
1 teaspoon gold magnetic sand
A pinch of earth from 5 banks
A lock of your hair
1 wishbone
3 hairs off a coconut

"MAGIC 3"
MOJO FOR LUCK

What you'll need:

> 1 teaspoon dirt from a crossroad
> 1 lodestone
> 1 silver nickel

"MORE THAN FRIENDS"
MOJO FOR LOVE

What you'll need:

    A picture of you and your friend
    A clipping of pubic hair
    2 magnets
    Hair or nail clippings from your friend
    1 moodstone

"PAYDAY"
MOJO FOR MONEY

INTO A SMALL GREEN drawstring bag place a lock of your hair, fingernail clippings, dirt from around a bank, five dried bay leaves, a penny, a nickel, a dime, and a quarter. Tie the bag securely and bury it for five days near a bank or any thriving business. Anoint with Money Drawing oil and carry it in your pocket or purse.

CONTACTS, SUPPLIES,
AND READINGS

IF YOU GO ONLINE and type in the word *Hoodoo*, you will get a list of suppliers that sell gris-gris bags, herbs, powders, oils, and other paraphernalia by mail. Many of the products come with inaccurate explanations and instructions for use. Most of them don't tell the consumer that the work is useless if it is not cleansed or personalized in one of the ways mentioned earlier. Note that few of these businesses are operated by a person familiar with Rootworking, although they may be initiated into an African traditional religion such as Vodun, Yoruba, or Palo Monte. Here are a few businesses and people I am familiar with.

Ava Kay Jones: Voodoo and Yoruba priestess. She prepares great gris-gris bags and oils the old fashioned way in New Orleans. (504) 866-3969.

Voodoo Authentica: This is a wonderful shop with very friendly people and real practitioners on staff. If you're in New Orleans make sure you drop by. They have a great selection of herbs to choose from. 201 N. Peters Street, New Orleans, LA 70130; Phone (504) 522-2111. Website: *voodooshop@aol.com*

FOR MORE INFORMATION

Here are a few websites I highly recommend:

www.afrikaworld.net This site is awesome for information on Africa and African-based religions/practices.

www.mamiwata.com This site gives the most accurate information on Vodun and the history/philosophy of African religious thought. One of the best on the web!

www.holisticonline.com Great information on herbs and their curative properties. A Rootworkers' dream come true!

GLOSSARY OF TERMS

Botanica—A shop specializing in occult supplies, especially in the implements used in African-based traditional religions.

Divination—The prediction of future events based on present circumstances, or using a tool or aid for that purpose.

Hoodoo—Also called Rootwork. An African-based system of healing and magick primarily using roots and herbs.

Maafa—Kiswahili term meaning "disaster" or "terrible occurrence," referring to the transatlantic slave holocaust.

Magick—When spelled with a "k" the term refers to something real that cannot be scientifically proven.

Mojo bag—A tiny bag worn against the skin that includes carefully prepared ingredients meant to achieve a particular objective. Also called "gris-gris."

Nation Sack—A mojo bag prepared by a woman for a woman used to achieve a particular goal, usually love or domination of a lover.

Rootworker—A person skilled in the use of herbs and roots to cure illness or cast spells.

Voodoo—A religion that originated in the ancient kingdom of Dahomey (present-day Benin) in West Africa and transported to the Carribbean and the Americas by African slaves. The proper name for this religion is Vodun, which means "Spirit" or "God" in the language of the Ewe/Fon tribe.

BIBLIOGRAPHY

Hyatts, Middleton Harry. *Hoodoo, Conjuration, Witchcraft, Rootwork.* Alma Egan Hyatt Foundation, 1935

The New York Public Library African American Desk Reference. Wiley, 1999

Henning, Christoph and Konemann Inc. staff, ed. *Soul of Africa: Magical Rites and Traditions.* Konemann, 1999

Glassman, Sallie Ann. *Vodou Visions.* Villard, 2000

INDEX

ABOUT THE AUTHOR

Tayannah Lee McQuillar studied anthropology at the City University of New York, and has studied the Magio-religious practices of black America. She has taught workshops on Astrology, Magick, Tarot, and African traditional religions.

She lives in New York City. Visit her at www.TayannahMcQuillar.com